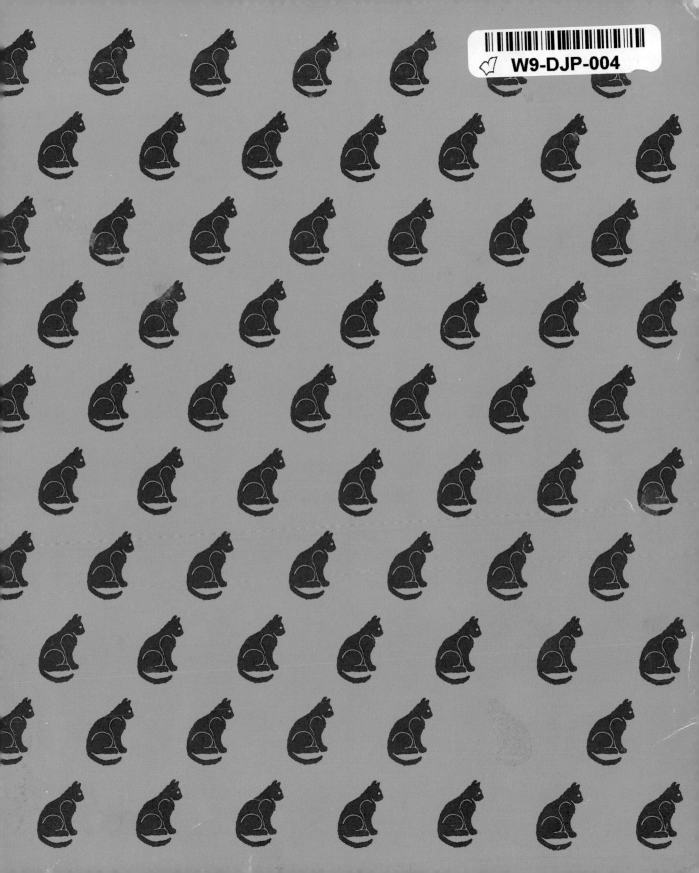

A Dorling Kindersley Book
Conceived, edited and designed by DK Direct Limited

Note to parents

What's Inside? Small Animals is designed to help young children understand what goes on inside the bodies of some of the strange and wonderful creatures around them. It shows them the intricate bone structure of a snake, how a frog's muscles are built for jumping, and the inner workings of a farmyard chicken. It is a book for you and your child to read and talk about together, and to enjoy.

Designers Sonia Whillock and Juliette Norsworthy
Typographic Designer Nigel Coath
Editors Simon Bell and Alexandra Parsons
Design Director Ed Day
Editorial Director Jonathan Reed

Illustrator Richard Manning
Photographer Andreas von Einsiedel
Writer Angela Royston
Animals supplied by Trevor Smith's Animal World
Additional editorial research by Trevor Smith's Animal World

SCHOLASTIC BOOK CLUB EDITION
First American Edition, 1991
Dorling Kindersley Inc., New York

Library of Congress Catalog Card Number: 91-60533

ISBN 0-590-46614-3

Printed in Italy

WHAT'S INSIDE?
SMALL ANIMALS

DORLING KINDERSLEY
NEW YORK
SCHOLASTIC BOOK CLUB EDITION

MOUSE

This mouse lives in a hole in the wall.

He has big ears, fine whiskers and a long tail.

Inside his body he looks like many other animals.

He has bones, muscles, a heart, a stomach and a brain.

His soft fur keeps him warm.

The mouse's large ears help him to hear even the smallest sounds.

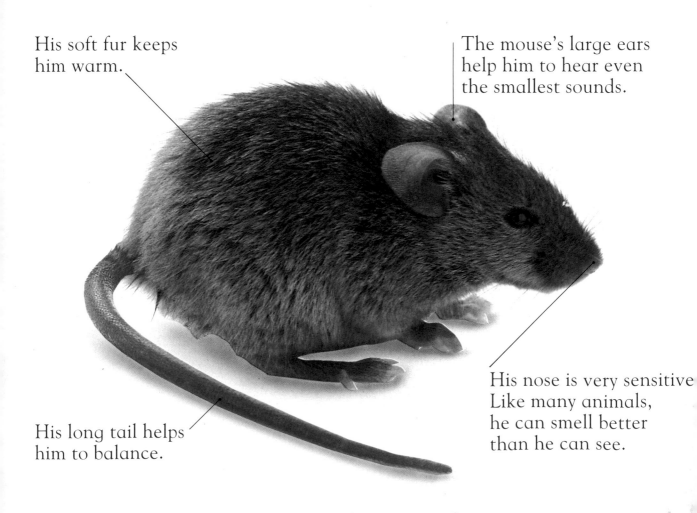

His long tail helps him to balance.

His nose is very sensitive Like many animals, he can smell better than he can see.

Do mice like cheese?
Not really; they would
rather eat candy.

This is his heart.
It is a strong muscle
that pumps blood.
It never stops working.

This is his backbone.
It runs from his neck
to the tip of his tail.
Bones give his body
its mouse shape.

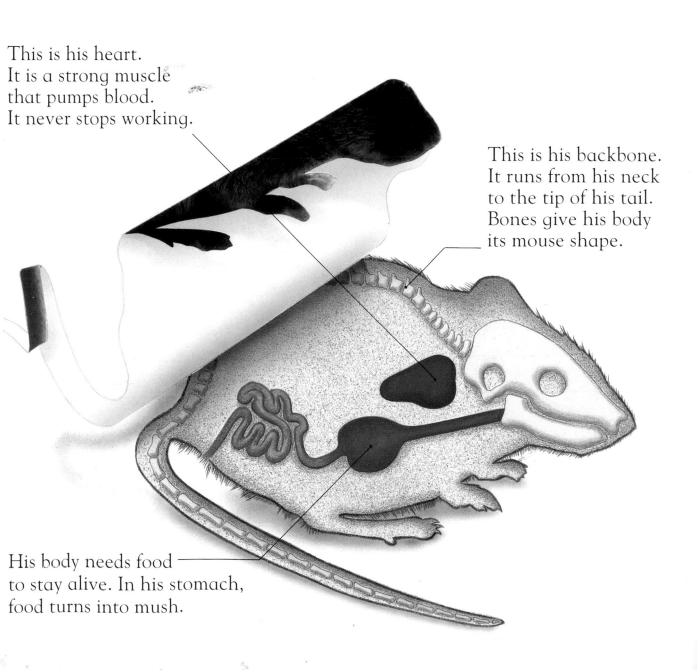

His body needs food
to stay alive. In his stomach,
food turns into mush.

3

SPIDER

Here is one of the biggest spiders in the world.
She is so big she can eat mice and small birds, but she
makes sure they are dead first by nipping them
with her poisonous fangs.

She has eight long legs
and eight beady eyes.

She has sensitive hairs
on her legs to help
her find her way.

These are called
spinnerets. This is
where the silk for her
web comes from.

Spiders have no bones.
Their skin is hard like a shell
to protect their insides.

Her food goes
into a kind of
stomach, called
a gizzard.

These are her fangs,
filled with poison.

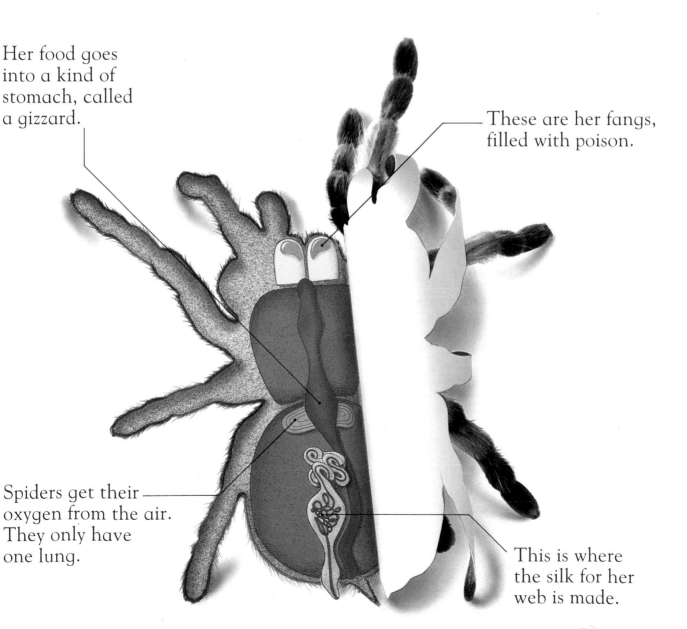

Spiders get their
oxygen from the air.
They only have
one lung.

This is where
the silk for her
web is made.

CHICKEN

This chicken is a bird, but she cannot fly.
She has feathers, wings and a beak like other birds.
She lays one egg almost every day.

She pecks her food with her beak.
Chickens have no teeth so
they swallow their food whole.

Strong outer feathers
keep the chicken's
body safe and dry.

She has strong
legs and long claws.
She uses these to
scratch the ground,
looking for things to eat.

Underneath she has
soft, downy feathers
to keep her warm.

Inside the egg there is
a bright yellow yolk.
The sticky liquid around it
is clear, like water.

Each egg is made inside her body.
The shell forms last of all, and
hardens just as she pushes
it out of her body.

This is the stomach.
Because they have no
teeth, chickens swallow
pieces of grit to help
grind up their food.

This is the crop.
Food is stored here
before it is passed
to the stomach.

7

GOLDFISH

This goldfish has shiny golden scales.
Like all fish, his body is smooth and pointed
at the front to help him slip through the water.

His scales are
hard and slimy.
They help to keep
his body safe
from harm.

This is his tail fin.
It helps him steer through
the water.

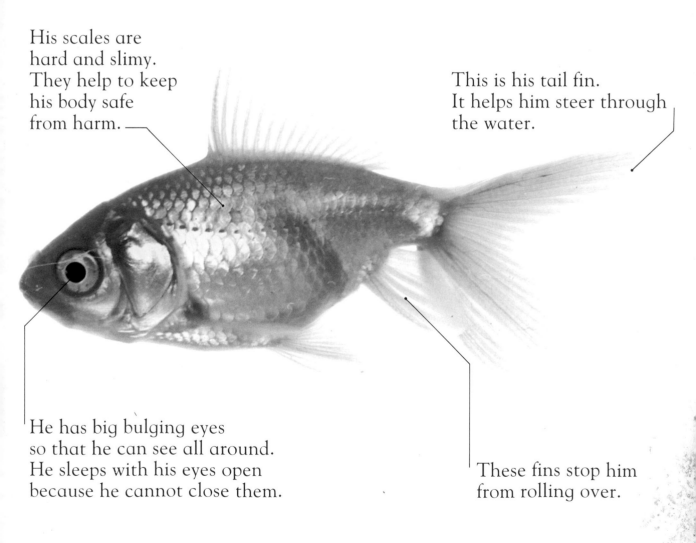

He has big bulging eyes
so that he can see all around.
He sleeps with his eyes open
because he cannot close them.

These fins stop him
from rolling over.

Fish do not breathe air.
Instead, they use their gills to get
the oxygen they need from water.

He uses these muscles to
move his backbone and fins.

His backbone is made
of many little bones
so he can twist and
turn as he swims.

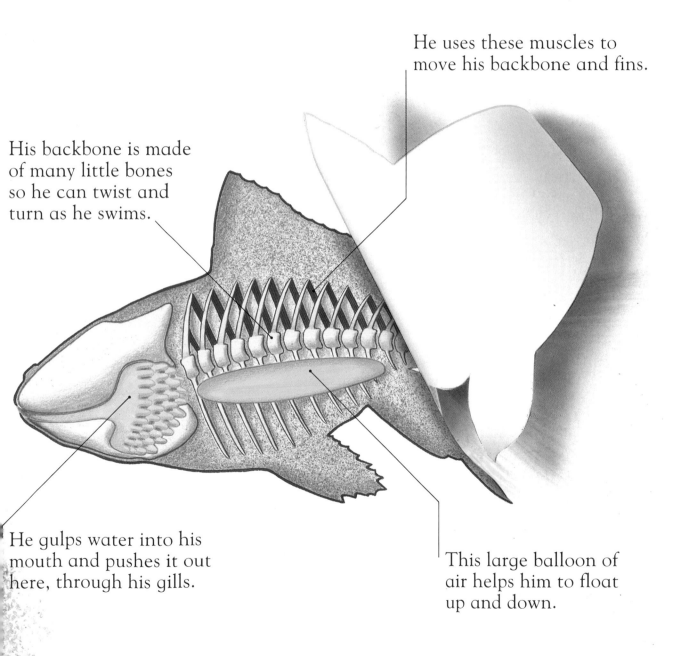

He gulps water into his
mouth and pushes it out
here, through his gills.

This large balloon of
air helps him to float
up and down.

CAT

Here is a small and friendly tabby cat.
She is part of the same family as big, fierce lions
and tigers. All cats are hunters.

She has large ears
so she can hear even
the tiniest sounds.

Like many
animals, she
sees the world
in black and
white, not
in color.

Her long tail helps
her balance as
she walks along
narrow walls
and ledges.

She has warm,
soft fur that
she licks clean
with her rough,
wet tongue.

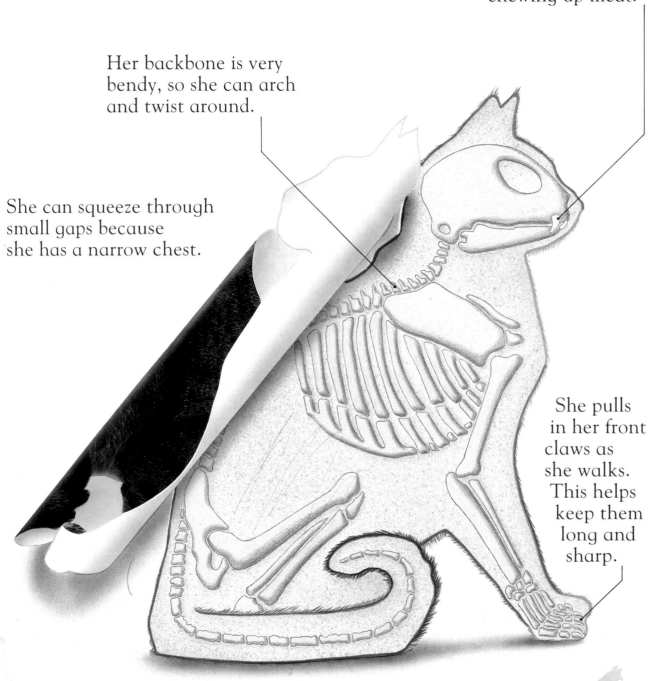

She uses her sharp teeth for tearing and chewing up meat.

Her backbone is very bendy, so she can arch and twist around.

She can squeeze through small gaps because she has a narrow chest.

She pulls in her front claws as she walks. This helps keep them long and sharp.

11

SNAKE

Here is a deadly rattlesnake. He lives in the desert.
Like all snakes he has no legs and his skin,
which is soft and dry to touch, is made of
tiny overlapping scales.

He cannot close his eyes,
because he has no eyelids.
His eyes are protected
by a layer of strong,
see-through skin.

His scales help him to
get a grip on the ground
as he wriggles along.

He doesn't have
a nose like you.
He flicks out his
long, forked tongue
to "taste" the air
for nearby food.

When he wants
to frighten his
enemies he shakes
his rattle loudly.

The only bones he has are his headbone, backbone and ribs – but he *does* have a lot of ribs!

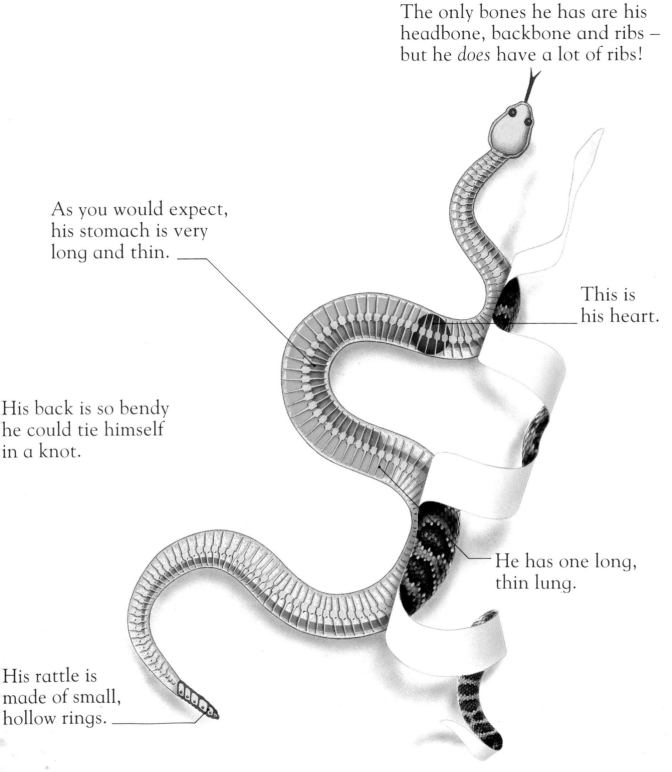

As you would expect, his stomach is very long and thin.

This is his heart.

His back is so bendy he could tie himself in a knot.

He has one long, thin lung.

His rattle is made of small, hollow rings.

FROG

This frog started life as a tiny tadpole living in a pond.
Now he is grown up and he can live and breathe
in the water and on the land. He must keep his skin damp
and so he likes wet, marshy places best.

He has big bulging eyes on
the very top of his head so he
can peep out of the water.

He gets the water he needs
through his thin skin,
not through his mouth.

His skin feels
cold and slimy.

He has back feet like
flippers to help him swim.

Frogs don't walk, they jump.
They have long bones and strong
muscles in their back legs. These help
them to jump a very long way.

He shoots out
his long tongue to
catch insects to eat.
The end is shaped
like a fork.

This is the frog's voice box.
He puffs out this bag of skin
to make his croak louder.

Frogs have lungs
but they also
get air into
their bodies
through
their skin.

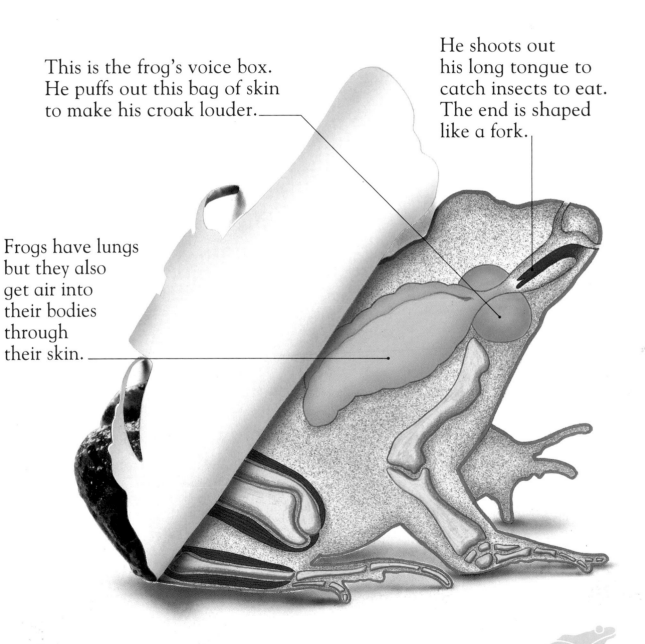

LIZARD

Lizards look like little crocodiles.
They live in dry, rocky places and there is nothing
they like more than sunbathing all day.

His body is flat and
thin so he can hide
in cracks in rocks.

His tough, spiny
scales are marked
to look like the
stony, sandy
ground where he
lives. They protect
him and hide him.

He can scuttle
away from danger
on his long, thin toes.

He waves his
tail angrily to
scare other
animals away.

Lizards don't have warm blood like we do. To warm up their insides they have to lie in the sun. To cool down they hide under rocks.

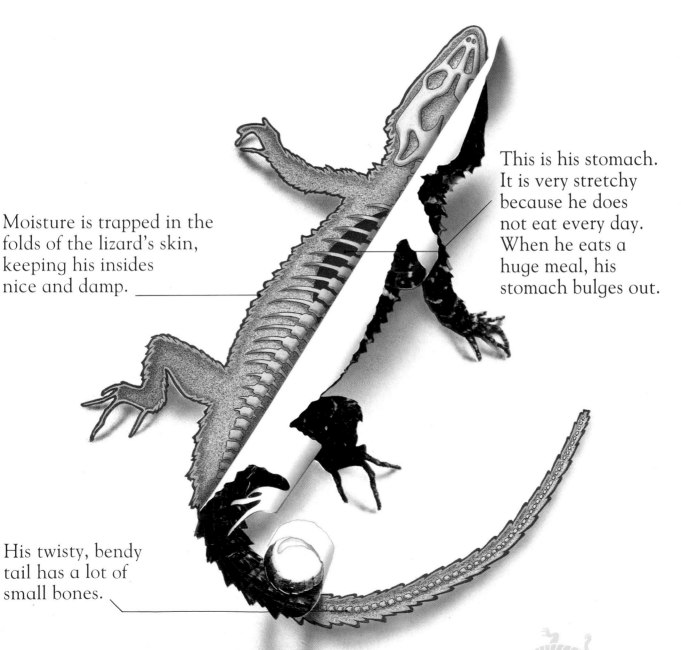

This is his stomach. It is very stretchy because he does not eat every day. When he eats a huge meal, his stomach bulges out.

Moisture is trapped in the folds of the lizard's skin, keeping his insides nice and damp.

His twisty, bendy tail has a lot of small bones.

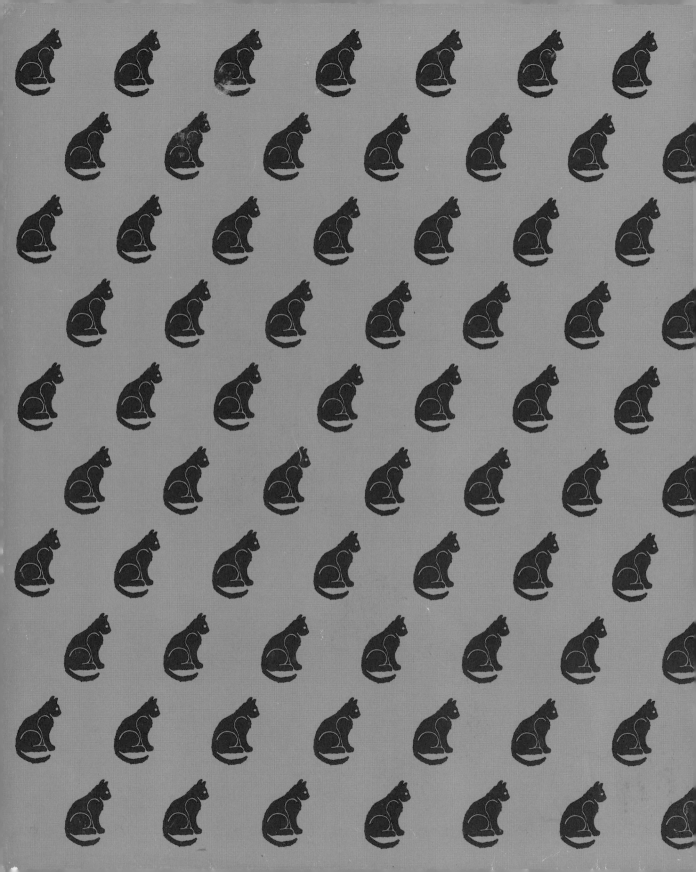